Formatting Notice

The voice of all of those who contributed recipes to this book has been preserved where possible, with the following exceptions.

Occasional spelling errors have been fixed.

Paragraphs may have been rearranged, for readability.

Measurements are provided in both imperial and metric forms where it is feasible to do so.

FOREWORD

Welcome! We are so glad to share some of our great food loves with you! This recipe book is a celebration of 85 years of St Thomas' Church, Ipswich, and a fantastic drawing together of culinary wisdom from many people who are connected with St Thomas', including recipes from congregation members, clergy past and present, and friends.

We are a vibrant and welcoming community. We love to share food. One of the things we do best at St Thomas' is eating together, so we invite you to join us through the collection of recipes and share in our hospitality, love and fun.

We think that Jesus gave us the best example. He was always eating with people. No matter their background, everyone was welcome to eat at the table with him. Some of Jesus' most memorable moments were sharing food - turning water into wine, feeding 5,000 people with loaves and fish, and passing bread and wine around the table to his disciples. Love, hospitality and food all go together as part of God's amazing plan for us all.

Most of us, probably, have food memories - foods that make us happy, that connect us with other people, that anchor us in a time or place. Maybe there's a smell that instantly transports you somewhere wonderful, or a particular dish you crave on a cold winter evening. Maybe you are a seasoned cook or baker, or perhaps you are just starting out. Maybe you love to be adventurous, or prefer to stick with tried and tested favourites!

But whatever place food has in your heart, we believe it is always better shared with others.

So this book is a way of sharing with you an offering of our favourite things to cook and eat, a gathering of all we love. We invite you to join our family, to sit at our table and eat.

– *The Rev'd Rachel Revely*

CONTENTS

Savoury Dishes

Great Recipes, No Doubt

Adrian's Cheese Scones
- Adrian Bullard

I love these scones, my wife added the red onion and mustard which makes them the best cheese scones ever! I think they are best served straight from the oven with the butter melting. My dear granddad loved these too and I am keeping up the family tradition.

<u>Ingredients</u>

225g (8oz) self raising flour
2.5ml (½ tsp) salt
50g (2oz) butter
150ml (¼ pint) fresh milk
1 tsp dry mustard
Pinch cayenne pepper
50g (2oz) grated English cheddar
Medium red onion, chopped
Extra milk for brushing

<u>Method</u>

Fry the chopped red onion and allow to cool.

Sift flour, mustard, cayenne pepper and salt into a bowl. Rub in butter until mixture resembles fine breadcrumbs.

Add in cheese and red onion.

Add milk. Mix to a soft dough.

Turn on to a lightly floured surface and knead until smooth.

Roll out to about 1 cm (½" thick) and cut into rounds.

Transfer to a greased baking sheet and brush tops with milk.

Bake at 230C / 450F / Mark 8 for around 7-10 minutes.

Then Jesus declared, "I am the bread of life. Whoever comes to me will never go hungry, and whoever believes in me will never be thirsty."

JOHN 6:35

Cheese Straws
– Sylvia Dickerson

Ingredients

100g / 4oz flour
¼ tsp dry mustard
¼ tsp salt
Shake of cayenne pepper
65g / 2½oz butter
50g / 1¾oz grated cheddar
1 egg yolk
10-15ml / 2-3 tsp cold water

Method

Sift flour, mustard, salt and pepper into a bowl.

Cut butter into flour and rub in until mixture resembles breadcrumbs.

Add cheese and mix ingredients together.

Mix to stiff paste with egg yolk and water.

Turn out on to a floured work surface and knead until smooth.

Wrap in foil and chill for 30 minutes.

Cook at 200°C / 400°F / Gas Mark 6.

Cheese Delight
– Marilyn Smith

<u>Ingredients</u>

2 eggs, well beaten
2oz / 57g margarine
2oz / 57g grated cheese
2oz / 57g wholemeal flour
1 breakfast cup cold water (equals ½ pint)
Salt and pepper

<u>Method</u>

Season the flour with salt and pepper. Add the cold water very gradually, mixing to a smooth cream.

Melt the margarine in a saucepan and add flour mixture. Stir and boil for 5 minutes.

Stir in the grated cheese and remove from the heat.

Add the well beaten eggs and pour into a well-greased baking dish.

Bake for 30 minutes.

Serve with green beans, either hot or cold as a salad.

Ham And Cheese Whirls
- Edith Abbott

Ingredients

1 packet puff pastry
1 packet ham
Grated cheese
Mustard

Method

Unroll puff pastry, spread with mustard, cover with ham and then with grated cheese.

Rolls up tightly, cut into small slices. Place on a greased baking tin and brush with egg.

Oven 200°C / Gas 6 approximately 10 minutes.

These can also be made with tomato puree instead of mustard and only grated cheese.

Cheese And Potato Pie
– Luke di-Benga

First I got out a chopping board, a saucepan, some potatoes and a little knife.

Next, I peeled ten potatoes, chopped them and popped them in the saucepan and left them to boil. Then I grated some cheddar cheese.

I prodded the potatoes to make sure they were soft – ready to mash. I drained the water out into a sieve and then poured the potatoes back into the saucepan.

I mashed them and added a block of butter and a little bit of mustard. Then I mixed them up altogether.

Finally I put the cheesy mash into a dish.

I make this at WotsUp day service for Mum and me to have for dinner.

You can also add other ingredients to the pie like mushrooms, peas, sweetcorn or ham/bacon.

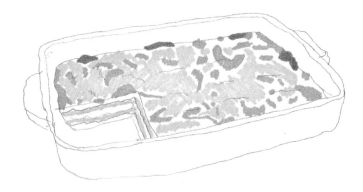

Priest's Perfect Puddings (Of The Yorkshire Variety)
– The Rev'd Rachel Revely

Ingredients

70g / 2½oz plain flour
2 eggs
100 ml milk
1 tbsp olive oil
Salt

Method

Preheat the oven to 220°C / 200°C for fan assisted / Gas 7.

Add half a tsp of olive oil to each of a 6 cup muffin tin and place into the hot oven.

Add the flour and eggs to large bowl and mix thoroughly

Gradually add the milk, ensuring each part is fully incorporated into the mix before adding more.

Season with salt (half a tsp).

Leave to rest till ready to cook (optional).

Remove the tray from the oven and carefully pour in the batter evenly distributed between the 6 holes.

Cook for 20-25 minutes until the Yorkshire puddings are puffed up and crisp.

Remove from the oven and serve immediately.

Fiona's Fave Feta Parcels
– Andrea McDonald

This is one of my successful recipes when it comes to feeding fussy Fiona.

Ingredients

1 pack of puff pastry (or filo pastry, as it's healthier and more often "stickered" in shops)
250g / 9oz feta
1 tub cottage cheese (makes it taste milder and the feta go further)

Method

Mix both cheeses together (and add spinach without telling the kids!)

Cut the puff pastry into squares.

Divide the mixture between squares and attempt to close them into parcels. But don't worry, they come apart again when baking.

Bake according to package instructions.

Goes with Greek salad, or any old salad really.

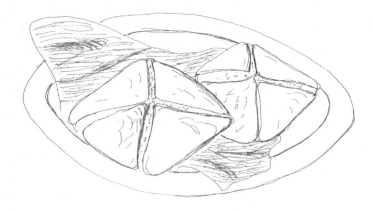

Breakfast Muffins
– The Rev'd Jackie Sears

<u>Ingredients</u>

8 eggs
Tomatoes, chopped
Pepper, chopped,
Mushrooms, sliced
Ham
Grated cheese

<u>Method</u>

Prepare muffin tin by spraying with low calorie cooking spray.

Whisk eggs together.

Mix the tomatoes, ham, pepper and mushrooms together and divide between the muffin tins.

Add the whisked eggs to the muffin tins making sure not to overfill.

Sprinkle grated cheese on top of each muffin.

Cook in oven for 20 mins 200°C / Gas 6.

Place on cooling tray. Refrigerate until required. Place in microwave for 30-50 seconds to reheat.

These can be used for breakfast or for lunch, topped with baked beans.

Ujeqe/South African Dumplings
– Smangele Ndlovu

Ingredients

6 cups of flour
10g / ¼oz instant yeast
¼ cup oil or melted butter
1 tsp salt
4 tbsp sugar
2 ½ cups warm water

Method

Mix ingredients together and knead until dough is soft and stretchy.

Using a large lidded saucepan, bring water to the boil. Rub ½ tsp of oil so the dough doesn't stick to the lid when it's risen.

Grease the bread tin with butter and put in the dough. Carefully place the tin into the saucepan, making sure the water isn't over the side of the tin. Steam for approximately one hour. You will know your bread is ready when you pierce through with the knife in the middle and the knife comes out clean.

The bread can be eaten with any curry or meats.

Holland Potatoes
- Mona Taylor

<u>Ingredients</u>

350g / 12¼oz potatoes (washed and sliced thinly)
500ml hot chicken stock
50g / 1¾oz butter

<u>Method</u>

Oven Gas No 6/ 200°C.

Grease a shallow ovenproof dish.

Arrange the sliced potatoes in the dish at a slight angle so they slightly overlap each other.

Pour over the hot stock. Dab the top with small knobs of butter.

Place on a baking tray.

Cover with foil.

Bake for 45 mins and then remove the foil and bake for 20-30 mins until golden.

Serve!

Nostalgic Scotch Eggs
- Mary Bullass

This recipe was passed on to me by one of the charities that I support. Given what St Thomas's Church stands for, it only seems fitting that I pass it on to all of you.

Ingredients

Two eggs
300g / 10½oz sausage meat
Two handfuls of breadcrumbs
Spray-on oil

Method

Soft-boil the eggs by making a hole in each of their shells and placing into boiling water for three-and-a-half minutes. Make sure the eggs are room-temperature; cold eggs are more likely to break in the heat.

Place the eggs in cold water to cool down after boiling, then remove the shells. Dry the eggs, then wrap them in the sausage meat.

Roll the meat-wrapped eggs in the breadcrumbs. Spray them with the oil and place on a baking sheet.

Cook for about twenty-five minutes at 180°C / 350°F / Gas 4, turning them over halway through cooking.

Stuffed Mushroom Caps
- Nigel Messenger

<u>Ingredients</u>

16oz / 453g fresh mushrooms
1tbsp butter
⅔ cup cooked chicken, chopped finely
¼ cup grated Parmesan cheese
1 tbsp fresh basil, chopped
2tsp lemon juice
⅛tsp onion powder
⅛tsp salt
Pinch of garlic powder
Pinch of black pepper
3oz / 85g cream cheese
Paprika, to garnish

<u>Method</u>

Preheat oven to 350°F / 180°C / Gas 4; grease a baking sheet.

Wash mushrooms; remove stems and finely chop. Arrange mushroom caps on the baking sheet smooth side down.

Melt the butter in a medium skillet over medium-high heat; add chopped mushroom stems and cook for five minutes while continuously stirring.

Add chicken, cheese, basil, lemon juice, onion powder, and the seasonings to the mixture. Cook and stir for another five minutes, then remove from heat and stir in the cream cheese.

Spoon the mixture into the hollows of each mushroom cap. Bake for 10-15 minutes or until heated through.

Garnish with paprika.

Crispy Bacon, Lentil And Avocado Salad
– The Ven. Rhiannon King, Archdeacon of Ipswich

Ingredients

50g / 1¾oz rocket
90g / 3¼oz smoked bacon
1 avocado
30g / 1oz feta
15g / ½oz pumpkin seeds
40g / 1½oz chilli jam/honey
15ml cider vinegar
400g / 14oz lentils, drained

Method

Prepare the avocado – cut in half and remove the stone. Scoop the avocado out of the skin and slice finely.

Heat a large non-stick pan over a medium high heat. Add the smoked streaky bacon and cook for 3-4 minutes on each side. Set aside.

Add the drained lentils to the non-stick pan with half the jam/honey, and season to taste with salt and pepper. Mix all together and warm through for 1-2 minutes.

Mix the remaining jam/honey with the cider vinegar and 1 tbsp oil, to make a dressing. Roughly chop the cooked bacon.

Mix together the hot lentils with the rocket and half the crispy bacon and transfer to dish. Top with the avocado. Crumble over the feta and drizzle over the dressing. Top with pumpkin seeds and the remaining bacon.

Broccoli Quiche
- Mona Taylor

<u>Ingredients</u>

Pastry:

200g / 7oz plain flour
100g / 3½oz butter/ margarine
Water to mix
Or half a packet of bought short crust pastry

Filling:

1 small onion finely chopped
2tsp olive oil
2 florets of cooked broccoli. cut into small pieces.
75g / 2½oz strong cheese, grated (stilton/blue cheese/cheddar)
2 eggs, beaten
75 mls milk
Freshly ground black pepper

<u>Method</u>

Light the oven Gas 6/ 200°C.

Make the pastry by rubbing the butter/ margarine into the flour to form breadcrumbs.

Add just enough water to bind it together.

Roll out on a floured surface to form a circle.

Line a 7" flan dish with the pastry.

Fry the chopped onion in the olive oil until soft.

Add the milk to the beaten eggs.

Place the onion and evenly in the flan case.

Cover with the grated cheese (save a little back for the top).

Pour over the egg mixture.

Sprinkle on the remaining cheese and black pepper.

Place on a METAL tray and bake for 20mins at Gas 6/200°C.

Turn down to Gas 4/180°C for another 20-25 minutes until golden brown and set.

Serve.

Better a small serving of vegetables with love than a fattened calf with hatred.

PROVERBS 15:17

Nutritious Vegetable & Chickpea Soup
– Lyanne Brendt

This is my preferred soup to serve at our Wellbeing Cafe. When I'm making it for there, I avoid potential allergens so don't use celery or celeriac, stock or salt. If I'm making it for home, I use whatever veg I can fit in. And I do use stock powder if I've got it.

I like to serve this as a smooth soup, so cook the veg in the oven, then heat it in my slow cooker at church. But if your slow cooker can have a stick blender in it, you could cook the whole thing in there. Mine can't...

Preheat your oven to 180°C / Gas 4 if needed. I've got a fan oven, & I put it on when the first pan goes in. Prep your veg:

Wash potatoes and cut into chunks to roast them. (Cut smaller if they're being cooked in the slow cooker, about 1.5cm dice size.) Put in a roasting tin and drizzle with oil. I use rapeseed oil. Put them in the oven (& turn it on if you've not already done so).

Scrub or peel 4 carrots and slice, put in a roasting tin... What else can you fit in there? More carrots? A cauliflower, cut into florets? Fill these tins up before they go in the oven! Also, drizzle with oil...

Onions and garlic - peel, cut onions into quarters or eighths, depending on how big they were. What else have you got? Brussels sprouts? Cabbage? Butternut squash? Prep it and cook it!

Once you've got all the veg cooking in the oven, set a timer, & have a tidy up & wash up. My oven takes 30 minutes to get it all cooked. You can get the washing on the line, or walk the dog, or read a good book. Oh, actually, could you make some angels for Christmas? You can get a few origami ones done while the veg cooks!

Veg done? Turn that oven off! But if its safe to do so, you could leave the oven ajar so you get the warmth from it.

Drain 1 or 2 cans of chickpeas. Aldi, Lidl & Morrisons do nice soft chickpeas, as do Napolina. But Napolina are a lot more money!

(You can also use dried chickpeas that you've soaked over night, rinsed and cooked carefully - boil uncovered for 10 minutes, then put the lid on, turn the hob down & simmer for 1 hour to 1 & 1/2 hours. I do 2 packs at a time in my stock pot, & freeze in recycled 400g yogurt tubs. So I'd use 1 or 2 yogurt tubs. But tins are easier. And you can keep the aqua faba liquid to use as egg replacer.)

Blend the veg & chickpeas. I put a tray at a time in my liquidiser and add water to make 1 litre, and blend. The smooth soup then goes into my slow cooker. Once all the veg & chickpeas are blended, I half fill the liquidiser and pulse to get all the veg out into the slow cooker (& help make it easier to wash it up). Give it a gentle stir to mix together. If I were making it for home, this is also where I'd add the stock & check to see if it needed more salt.

Carefully take to church & plug the slow cooker in. Heat thoroughly, & serve with ordinary rolls & gluten-free rolls, & dairy free margarine.

"Chuck It All In" Soup
- Keri Harrison and Sue Dickerson

<u>Ingredients</u>

Any vegetables of choice
Stock

<u>Method</u>

Chop veg up and add to the pan.

Make stock up according to its instructions; add one more stock cube for flavour if desired.

Boil until the veg becomes soft.

Add to blender and whizz away until desired texture is reached.

Lucy's Cauliflower Soup
– Lucy Drake

This is a really easy and delicious soup which is tangy and mildly spicy, and doesn't taste overpoweringly of cauliflower. All ingredients are approximate and can be varied depending what you have and the flavours you like, or don't. It makes a large quantity of soup – maybe enough for 8-10 servings – so use a big saucepan! Good to make in advance as it is even better the next day, and will keep for several days.

Ingredients

A large onion
A piece of root ginger, about 5cm by 2cm
Oil
1 heaped teaspoon turmeric powder
1 heaped teaspoon fennel seeds
1 cauliflower
2 medium or 1 large potato
A lemon
25-50g / 1-1¾oz dried, finely shredded coconut
1 heaped teaspoon Bouillon powder
Salt

Method

Peel and chop the onion coarsely and the root ginger very finely.

Put a good slug of any cooking oil you have in a large saucepan, throw in the onions and ginger and cook on a medium heat with the lid off, stirring from time to time. Carry on cooking and stirring for about 5 mins or until the onion has softened but not gone brown.

While that's cooking, cut off the base of the stem and leaves from the cauli (if they are in good shape save them to use as a separate veg) and break/cut the florets off the stem, cutting the larger ones into smaller pieces so they are all roughly the same size. Chop up the stalk as well.

Peel and chop the potatoes into roughly 1cm cubes, or smaller.

While you are doing that, boil a half-full kettle.

Put the turmeric and fennel seeds into the saucepan and stir around for a minute.

Add the cauli pieces and stir everything around for another minute trying to get as much of the cauli coloured with the spices as you can. You don't want to burn the spices or cauli as the flavour is horrid.

Add the potato cubes (no need to mix). Add the bouillon powder if you are using it.

Add the boiled water to just cover the veg. Watch out as the cauli will float. It doesn't matter if some of it is above the water as it will cook in the steam. You are aiming for a thick soup so use the minimum amount of water.

Squeeze the lemon and add half the juice to the pan, or all of it if you like lemon. Alternatively you can decide at the end if you want more lemon. It is a key ingredient which really transforms the soup.

Throw in as much dried coconut as you want. This is not essential but adds a nutty taste/texture. If you really like coconut you could use coconut milk instead of some of the water.

Put the lid on the pan and simmer. Check after 10 mins if the potato pieces are soft. They may need a few minutes longer but you don't want to overcook the cauli which ideally should have a slight 'bite' to it.

Liquidise the soup in 2 batches till it is smooth. Add more water only if needed.

Taste and add salt / more lemon juice as needed. Yummy served with plain yoghurt.

"Tattie" Soup With Croutons
- The Rev'd Canon Christopher Chapman

This recipe comes from my mother, who was born in 1904 of a Scots father and a second generation Irish immigrant mother, and who was in domestic service in Kent until her marriage, so I have no idea where the recipe may have originated! The use of the word "tattie" for potatoes may indicate a Scottish origin, but not necessarily! It is a fairly thick soup, and therefore can be used as a nutritious main course if served with a bread roll or croutons.

Ingredients

Hock ham bones (these are sold in some East of England Coop shops for about £3.00)
Two medium or one large onion
4 medium sized potatoes
2 or 3 carrots
1 medium sized swede
1 or 2 parsnips
1 dessert spoon of mixed herbs (fresh or dried)
Black pepper to taste
Slow cooker or large saucepan
Hand or electrical grater

For the croutons:
3 or 4 slices of sliced wholemeal bread, diced
Three tablespoons of cooking oil
Frying pan

Method

Remove the hock bones from their packaging and place in a slow cooker or large saucepan. Cover with cold water, add the herbs, cover the pot and bring to the boil, turn down the heating and simmer for an hour or so, then turn off the heating.

Remove the bones and meat from the pot, allow to cool

sufficiently to handle comfortably, strip the meat from the bones and if necessary cut into small pieces and return to the pot.

Peel the potatoes, carrots, swede and onions, cut into chunks and grate into the pot.

Peel the parsnips, cut into quarters lengthwise, remove the 'woody' centre and dispose with the peelings, grate the parsnips into the pot.

Add the pepper to taste,

Cover the pot and return it to a low heat and simmer for two hours, stirring regularly. Serve immediately or pack into boxes with lids and allow to cool before freezing.

For the croutons: heat the cooking oil in a frying pan, and fry the diced bread till crisp, remove from the pan, drain on crumpled kitchen roll until cool.

Serve in small bowls to be sprinkled on the soup when served and enjoy!

Potato Soup
– Andrea McDonald

<u>Ingredients</u>

1 kg / 35oz potatoes
1.5 litres / 53 fl oz water
Add
1 small celeriac
1 large onion
2-3 carrots
If you feel adventurous add ½ bulb of fennel

<u>Method</u>

Put every thing in a slow cooker and cook.

Pushed for time? Use a pressure cooker. It also keeps its flavour nicely.

He gives food to every creature. His love endures forever.

PSALM 136:25

Noodle Soup
– Lyanne Brendt

We first had noodle soup when Aaron made it at school. It's a silly recipe to do at school and send home, the noodles keep absorbing the liquid and become very overcooked. But as a recipe to do at home, it's good. It's very good for fighting off colds. But it can be a pain to make when you're the one feeling ill. Aaron had a brain wave! Make a lot of the soup base and freeze in small portions, so you can finish cooking from frozen, and add the noodles so they're just right for you to eat.

This is a lot easier with a food processor to prep the large amounts of veg. But there's no reason not to do it by hand, and the veg will look more appealing if you do that.

Fresh ginger. Fresh chillies. 2 bulbs of garlic (not 2 little cloves, 2 nice big chunky bulbs with lots of cloves in them). I used ginger and chillies from the top up shop.

Prep these 3 - it's easiest to peel ginger with a little teaspoon, it sounds weird, but it really works. Wash the chillies - be careful if you're a contact lens wearer! Peel the papery skin of the many garlic cloves.

They all need cutting up finely. If you're using the food processor, cut or break the ginger into 2cm-ish pieces, and throw them all in. Or finely grate the ginger and garlic, and carefully chop the chilli. I've got a fancy hachoir thing I won in a raffle, and it's brilliant for chillies, because I don't have to touch them.

Onion - lots... About 3 large, to 6 small. Or more if they need using up. Peel and roughly quarter to put in the food processor. Or finely slice.

If you're using the food processor, add a shot glass of water. Or a dinky little measuring cup that's the same size as a shot glass. Or 2 tablespoons. You just need a bit of water, to help it all blend finely. Now blend it till you can't see any chunks of spicy spicy veg.

Carrots - again, 3 large to 6 small, more if they need using up... They look best julienned. But coarsely grated works fine too. So get them shredded.

Get a big saucepan, and start heating some oil in it. I like 'stir fry oil' from the supermarket, which is a mix of sunflower oil & sesame seed oil (delicious, but a common allergen) with ginger and garlic extracts. But you use what you've got & heats well. Olive oil is not your friend here.

As the oil heats up, finely slice some peppers - red and yellow will look good, you won't really see orange against the carrot. You can also use green, but we don't like that as much as the riper, sweeter peppers. But use what you've got!

Add the prepped veg to the hot oil. You could add salt, but I don't as I like to add soy sauce before eating the soup. I do like to add Chinese 5 spice mix to it though - about 2 teaspoons. But don't go and buy it just for this!

Cook the veg till it's soft. Stir it from time to time so it doesn't stick to the pan. It shouldn't take more than 10 minutes.

Let it cool down. If you've got a cupcake tin, this will be perfect to make nice little chunks of soup base. If you use your silicone cup cake cases, you'll think "yay, I'm so clever" as the soup base pops out of them so easily. And then, you'll wash them up, and discover they still smell of spicy garlicky soup. Delicious, but not in cupcakes. Anyway, divide the soup base into small portions. I find 1 cup of base is right for soup for 1 person, but if you can freeze it in smaller portions, that's better, as it will cook quicker. Freeze the portions, keep in the freezer.

To serve, take a small lidded saucepan, add 1 cup worth of frozen soup base (3 cupcake shapes...) and a mug of water and bring to the boil. Add a nest of noodles (I like to break the nest up first, you don't want to be fighting with the noodles when you need this soup). I use thick wholewheat noodles, so bring the soup back to the boil, turn the heat off and leave for 5 minutes to cook the noodles. But if you use fine rice noodles, they'll be done by the time you've stirred them into the soup. Pour into a bowl, maybe add some soy sauce and get yourself a glass of water while it cools down a little. Now eat all that soup. You need to help your body fight off those germs! Go and rest now, someone else can do the washing up, you're ill and need to take care of yourself.

Main Meals

Feed Me Now And Evermore

Tofu, Broccoli & Mushroom Stir Fry
– Lyanne Brendt

I'm glad to see you're feeling better now. But remember to eat lots of fruit and vegetables to help stay healthy! I usually serve this with noodles, but you can use rice instead. Check the cooking times for your rice, because it probably needs starting before the stir fry. A sachet of microwave rice would be good though, & use less energy to cook than noodles.

I use a big wok with a lid for this, because it's what I've got. If you haven't got one, use a big saucepan. Don't rush out and buy one!

I like Sainsburys' own tofu from their vegetarian chilled foods, because it's cheaper than the branded ones usually.

Prep your veg:
Slice one or two onions.
Cut the florets off a head of broccoli so they're fairly small and equal. And slice the stalk too, fight food waste when you can!
Slice mushrooms, cheap ones. I prefer chestnut mushrooms to white mushrooms, but get what's cheapest. I use between 250g to 400g / 9oz to 14oz mushrooms for this, I like mushrooms!
You can also add julienned carrots and sliced peppers. Use what you've got that needs using up!

If you got baby corn and mangetout from the top up shop, they'd be great in this. I mean, you can buy them of course, but they're pricey! Worth looking at in the supermarket though, as they're also often reduced.

Heat some oil in your wok or saucepan. I use stir fry oil (allergy warning! Contains sesame) but you could use any bland oil. Or peanut oil, if you've got it, but there's even more allergy warning for that. Put the veg into the hot oil & stir.

Put water on for noodles. Open the tofu pack over the sink as it's in water that goes on you & the floor if you're not careful. Cut it up

- I stand it on end and slice the block into 3 thick slices, then put them on the chopping board and slice into chip size pieces, then half those so the tofu pieces are a similar size to the broccoli & mushroom slices. Tofu is ready to eat, though very bland, so you're going to add it to the almost cooked veg too heat it through while you make the sauce.

Get a small bowl and crush 2 - 4 cloves of garlic into it. Add a teaspoon size amount of fresh ginger if you've got it, or an ice cube amount of frozen ginger, or half a teaspoon of dried ginger. Add a finely chopped fresh chilli, or the same amount of frozen chilli, or 1/4 - 1/2 teaspoon of dried chilli (I like chilli flakes, but use what you've got) - and if you don't like chilli, don't use it.

Add 1 tablespoon of cornflour, a teaspoon of stock powder or 1/2 a stock cube, and give it all a stir before adding liquid. 1 teaspoon of soy sauce (it's salty, you can add more, but not take it out!) & 1 teaspoon of sesame oil (allergy warning), and about 60 ml of cold water. Stir again and pour into the wok & give everything a good stir.

While you were making the sauce, the water should have boiled - add 1 noodle nest for each adult you're feeding. Wholewheat noodles take about 5 minutes, but you can turn the heat off from both rings so they cook with the residual heat. (This might not work so well with gas. Know your cooker and use it as is best for you and your pocket!)

Drain the cooked noodles (we stir a bit of sesame oil into them before serving, but that's optional!) and serve, give the stir fry a last stir and pile onto the noodles.

Any leftovers taste delicious the next day for packed lunch.

Sunrise Salad For 4
– Karen Irwin

<u>Ingredients</u>

½ red sweet pepper
½ yellow sweet pepper
½ green sweet pepper
½ large carrot
½ punnet of baby plum tomatoes
50 grams red grapes
50 grams blueberries
50 grams pomegranates seeds
1 beetroot – preferably raw so can be cooked for this salad
Salad leaves as per your choice but these are my favourites as they are very tasty - large handful of rocket, large handful of pea shoots, large handful of baby spinach
You can add protein as per your choice - cooked chopped chicken, cottage or grated cheese or flaked cooked salmon

<u>Method</u>

If you have raw beetroot: chop into ½ inch cubes, space them out & pop onto a non-sick baking tray and put into the oven for about 45mins at 150°C / Gas 2.

The beetroot will need to cool totally before adding to the salad, so doing this the day before is fine. Raw beetroot that you cube and cook will have sealed edges so won't colour your food, also the flavour is much more intense, definitely worth the effort!

If you have pre-cooked beetroot: chop into cubes but keep separate from everything else until you're ready to serve.

Pre-cooked beetroot will be much wetter and will colour your salad red so leave separate until the last moment.

Slice all the sweet peppers so they are the length of the pepper giving more shapes and interest to the look of your salad.

Grate the carrot. Halve the baby plum tomatoes. Halve the red grapes.

Mix all the fruits & veg together along with your protein of choice, leaving the salad leaves for the moment.

If you have cooked your beetroot add it to the mix. If you have pre-cooked beetroot, do nothing with it for the moment.

Add your salad leaves to your serving bowl, or individual plates. On top of your leaves add the mixed salad fruits & veggies & protein.

If using pre-cooked beetroot sprinkle over the top.

Drizzle a small amount of olive oil over everything.

Vegan Chilli
– The Rev'd Jackie Sears

This is sometimes called "Pantry Chilli" as you can use what you have rather than go out and buy ingredients. I like my vegetables crunchy; if you prefer yours softer then add them after the onion and garlic.

<u>Ingredients</u>

450g / 16oz soy or vegetable mince
1 can red kidney beans
2-3 peppers
2 carrots
2 celery sticks
Tin chopped tomatoes
Tomato puree or passata
1 cube vegetable stock (or red wine)
2 onions
2 cloves garlic
2 tsp paprika or smoked paprika
1-2 fresh chilli pepper
Salt to taste
Optional – sweet potato or more beans

<u>Method</u>

Finely chop the vegetables.

Heat some olive oil in a saucepan over a medium heat. Add the onion and garlic and fry until soft.

Add the spices, soy mince and tomato puree/passata.

Cook for 3-4 minutes, stirring occasionally.

Add the chopped tomatoes and the stock. Stir well. Cook for another 3-4 minutes and bring to the boil.

When the mix starts bubbling, lower the heat and simmer for another 3-4 minutes.

Add the chopped peppers, celery and carrots. Stir well and cook for a few minutes.

Add the kidney beans. Mix well and simmer for a further few minutes.

This can be served with sour cream or vegan yoghurt, fresh herbs and lime. You can use with rice or quinoa as a chilli sin carne or as a topping for a baked potato or filling for a tortilla. Or serve with sweet potato chips or corn chips and add cheese (dairy free if using as vegan) - a bit like nachos.

Three Bean Chilli
– The Ven. Rhiannon King, Archdeacon of Ipswich

Ingredients

3 cloves garlic, crushed
1 tsp cumin seeds
185g / 6½oz butter beans
185g / 6½oz black beans
400g / 14oz red kidney beans
1 large onion, chopped
200g / 7oz passata/chopped tomatoes
40g / 1½oz chipotle paste
11g / ½oz vegetable stock mix
2 tsp smoked paprika

Method

Preheat the oven to 220°C / Gas 7.

Drain and rinse the beans. Mix together the drained beans, smoked paprika, cumin seeds, passata, onion and chipotle paste. Sprinkle in the veg stock cube. Heat a large pan with a drizzle of olive oil. Add the crushed garlic and 250ml boiled water and bring to the boil over a high heat.

Put mixture into a lidded casserole dish and place in the oven for 45-50 minutes until the chilli has thickened.

This can be served with jacket potatoes, or could be served with rice.

Sweet Potato And Spinach Curry
- Keri Harrison and Sue Dickerson

Ingredients

1 bag of sweet potatoes
1 bag of baby leaf spinach
Curry powder
2 tins of chopped tomatoes
Vegetable stock

Method

Cut potatoes into chunks and boil in stock.

Add tomatoes. Add curry powder - 1-2tsp, or more depending on your taste.

Add spinach and mix until wilted.

Simmer for 10-15 minutes, then serve with rice.

Mapo Tofu
– The Right Rev'd Martin Seeley, Bishop of St Edmundsbury & Ipswich

This is a very popular meal in our household, and I prepare it for whoever is home a couple of times a month. It is quite spicy, though you can control how spicy by whether you add chili oil. We get all the Chinese ingredients at Go East on Tacket Street where the staff are very helpful. Of course you can get tofu in most supermarkets, though you'll need to go to Go East if you want the softer silky variety. If you have a wok, that is ideal, but you can do this in a large frying pan. Eat with rice, and maybe some sauted pak choi.

Ingredients

Oil to fry in (I use olive or sunflower)
1 ½ tbsps ground Sichuan peppercorns
3 tbsps finely chopped fresh ginger
3 tbsps finely chopped garlic
200g / 7oz (or thereabouts) pork mince
1-2 tbsps. (depending on how spicy you want it) spicy bean sauce (comes in a plastic jar and called "chili paste with broad beans" – though in Chinese)
200mls chicken stock – low salt – we make our own from chicken bones
500g / 17½oz tofu cut into 2cm cubes
1 ½ tsps cornflour
2 spring onions white and pale green parts sliced
Chili oil

Method

Heat a lug of oil and add the ground Sichuan pepper, stirring for 30 seconds, and then add the ginger and fry for a minute, and then the garlic and fry for another minute, stirring occasionally. Add the pork mince, breaking it up and cooking it through.

Add the spicy bean sauce and stir in well so the colour is mixed through everything else. Then add the chicken stock and simmer. Mix the cornflour with a little water and pour in, stirring while it thickens.

This is the point to add the chili oil if you want it. Then add the tofu and gently mix it in so it is all coated with the sauce. Cook it all for a few minutes. Then put the spring onion slices on top and serve. You can add a little more ground Sichuan pepper if you like that numbing sensation it gives you!

Macaroni Cheese
– Keri Harrison and Sue Dickerson

Ingredients

Macaroni
Extra mature cheese
Tin of Campbell's tomato soup
Chopped onion
Black pepper
1tsp English mustard
Salt for the water

Method

Cook macaroni in saltwater and chopped onion. When cooked, the macaroni needs to be drained.

Heat a tin of Campbell's tomato soup, adding the amount of water suggested on the soup tin. When the soup is heated, add the mustard, black pepper to taste, and the grated cheese.

Return the cooked macaroni to the sauce. Mix together in the pot.

Serve with home-cooked chips in beef dripping.

Chorizo And Pasta
– Daphne Startup

<u>Ingredients</u>

Chorizo ring
Pasta
Bacon
Red and yellow pepper
Mushrooms
Red onions
Garlic
Sweetcorn
Peas
Passata
Tomato puree
Smoked paprika
Salt and black pepper
Anything else tasty!

Quantities are not crucial so just adjust to number of people wanting to try it.

<u>Method</u>

Chop all vegetables and chorizo and bacon. Fry everything.

Boil pasta. Mix all together.

Add sweetcorn, peas, passata, tomato puree, smoked paprika, salt and pepper. Bring to boil and simmer for 10 minutes. Enjoy!!

Baked Spaghetti With Meatballs
– Naomi Bloomfield

<u>Ingredients</u>

24oz / 680g jar marinara sauce (I used San Marzano sauce)
½ yellow onion (diced)
3 cloves garlic (crushed)
1 tsp Italian seasoning
2 tbsp olive oil
¾ pack spaghetti noodles
1-2 cups / 128-256g / 4½-9oz grated cheese (I used half Colby-jack, half mozzarella)
½ cup / 64g / 2¼oz grated parmesan
Homemade precooked meatballs of your choice (I used around 1½ dozen)

<u>Method</u>

In a large cast-iron skillet, sauté onions in olive oil over a med/low heat. Add in garlic and continue sautéing until onions are tender.

Add cooked meatballs.

Add marinara sauce and Italian seasoning.

In a separate large pot, cook spaghetti noodles according to package instructions (undercook by 2 minutes).

With a large slotted spoon, scoop meatballs from sauce and set aside.

Add cooked spaghetti to marinara sauce. Add in about ½ cup of the pasta cooking water. Gently stir until pasta is fully coated with sauce. Add cooked meatballs to top of spaghetti. Top with grated cheese and parmesan cheese.

Bake at 350°F / 180°C / Gas 4 for approx 20-30 minutes or until hot and bubbly and the cheese is melted.

Blessed are those who hunger and thirst for righteousness, for they will be filled.

MATTHEW 5:6

Vegan Butternut Squash Mac
- The Rev'd Lawrence Carey

<u>Ingredients</u>

1 onion (quartered)
1 butternut squash
30g / 1oz cashew nuts
35g / 1¼oz nutritional yeast
1 tsp dried rosemary
1 tsp mustard
1 veg stock cube (mixed into 480ml boiling water)

<u>Method</u>

Cut both ends off the butternut squash, poke it all over with a fork. Microwave on high for 3 minutes.

Peel the skin off the squash (it should peel easily once microwaved). Slice it in half lengthwise, scoop out the seeds, then cut into 2cm cubes.

Add butternut squash and the rest of the ingredients into slow cooker, stir to combine.

Turn on to low for 8 hours.

Once cooked, put mixture into a blender and puree for 5 minutes, until the sauce is thick and creamy.

Serve with macaroni.

Lamb And Halloumi Meatballs
– Sam Griggs

This is a lovely low fat recipe that Robyn has made over and over. It was the first dinner she ever made entirely on her own and made it better than me! She has perfected cooking spaghetti to go with it too.

Ingredients

500g / 17½oz lamb mince
125g / 4½oz halloumi cheese, diced into small cubes
2 tsps dried oregano
1 tsp paprika
1 onion, finely diced
3 cloves of garlic, crushed
1 400g / 14oz tin chopped tomatoes
150ml / 5fl oz / ⅔ cup chicken stock
8 fresh basil leaves

Method

Preheat the oven to 200°C fan / 425°F / Gas mark 7.

Mix together the lamb mince, halloumi, 1 tsp oregano and the paprika, being careful not to overmix.

Divide the mixture into 20-24 portions and roll them into meatballs.

Spray a large baking sheet with a little oil and place the meatballs on the sheet. Bake in the oven for 20 minutes.

Meanwhile place a large saucepan over a medium heat, spray with a little oil and add the onion. Cook for 2-3 minutes, until it is starting to turn translucent. Add the garlic and stir well, then add the rest of the ingredients to the pan. Bring to the boil, then reduce the heat and simmer for 10-15 minutes, until thickened.

When the meatballs are ready, add them to the pan and cook for another 10 minutes.

Vegetarian Lentil Bolognese
- The Rev'd Lawrence Carey

If you've got extra veggies then you could put in spinach, mushrooms, peppers, courgette, pretty much anything you fancy.

<u>Ingredients</u>

200g / 7oz lentils
2 carrots
3 celery sticks
250g / 8¾oz tomato passata
2 onions
400 ml vegetable stock (1 stock cube in boiling water)
1 tin chopped tomatoes
Mixed herbs
Salt & pepper to taste

<u>Method</u>

Follow instructions on lentils, some may say pre-soak them, some say no need to.

Chop and put in onions, carrots, celery and bit of salt and pepper and a splash on water or veg stock so that there is a bit of liquid for veggies to 'sweat' into the slow cooker.

Cook on high.

After 30 minutes, take lid off and give it a good stir, then add the rest of the ingredients (if you've had to pre-soak your lentils then drain the water off before adding them). Give it a good stir and leave on high for 2 – 3 hours or low for 4 – 6 hours, depending on how soft you like your carrots.

Serve with pasta, or anything you like.

Fish Pie With Sliced Potato Topping
– Gloria Elmer

I adapted this recipe from several fish pie recipes because we like the sliced potato topping rather than mashed potato. Also I have gone off meat but I have always loved fish.

It can be made with any kind of fish but the smoked haddock just gives it the edge.

<u>Ingredients</u>

1 pint / 568ml milk
1lb / 453g mixed fish (smoked haddock, salmon, cod loin)
1 onion
1 bay leaf
3 cloves (optional)
1 tbsp olive oil
3 tbsp plain flour
3oz / 85g raw king prawns
2oz / 57g frozen peas
1 lemon, grated zest only
1 tbsp finely chopped parsley
2 large potatoes sliced and par boiled.

<u>Method</u>

Heat the milk in a large pan and then add the fish. Cut the onion in half, put the cloves in same half and place this into the pan with the milk and fish. Add the bay leaf. Bring the milk to the boil, then reduce the heat and simmer gently for 6/7 minutes.

Meanwhile finely chop the remaining half onion. Heat the butter with the olive oil in a small frying pan and gently fry the onion for 4/5 minutes until softened but not browned. Remove the fish from the pan and set aside to cool slightly.

Keep the milk in the pan. Add the flour to the onion and stir well. Fry for 1 minute stirring frequently. Gradually spoon in the milk from poaching the fish and stir it in well each time. Taste the sauce for seasoning, adding salt or pepper as necessary (I just add garlic powder).

Break the fish into chunks, removing any bones and skin, then fold the fish pieces into the sauce. Add the raw prawns and frozen peas to the mixture, place into an ovenproof pie dish. Sprinkle the parsley and lemon zest over the top.

Carefully top with par boiled sliced potatoes and dot with the rest of the butter. Cook for 25-30 minutes until golden brown.

You might think fish pie always has mashed potato like we did, but Gloria's fish pie uses sliced potato to make it so delicious.

'Whatever You Like' Pie
- Alison Gibbs

I call this my "whatever you like pie" as you can use whatever you like – any sort of mince, soup or crisps. Garlic can be used when cooking rice, sweetcorn with or instead of peas; and any sort of vegetables can be used, but remember they will be crunchy.

Ingredients

Mince
Tin of mushroom soup
Chopped onion
Frozen peas
Fresh pepper, chopped
Sliced carrot
Mashed potato
Packet of crisps
Cheese

Method

Brown mince with some of the onion then place in an ovenproof dish.

Add a layer of frozen peas on top.

Pour over the tin of mushroom soup.

Add a layer of peppers, layer of carrots and the rest of the chopped onion.

Add mashed potato on top, then the cheese.

Cook in the oven for about 20 minutes.

Crush the crisps and place on top of melted cheese and put back in the oven for a minute or two.

Serve as it is or with garlic bread.

Bung It One Pot Chipotle Mince
– Jean Maxwell

There are no exact measurements for this bung it very basic mince meal with a bit of a kick! Adapt and make it your own.

You need a large pan (ideally wide but not tall, with a lid!).

Gently fry, in a little rapeseed oil, some shallots (I cry less than with onions) and after a little while add some garlic.

When all is softish spoon in some ready made chipotle paste - it's hot! I use about a dessert spoonful for a few portions. Cook for a minute.

Add some mince - I use turkey mince but any would do, stir and cook for a bit.

Add tins(s) of tomatoes, and a tin of kidney beans (or whatever is in the cupboard).

Add loads of chopped veg - root veg works well - carrots, parsnip, swede, turnip etc.

Add salt and pepper if you must - I don't!

Leave to bubble away. You may need to add some water to stop it drying out.

Nice on its own, lovely with a baked potato.

Mince Two Ways
– Andrea McDonald

If you have one 500g / 17½oz pack of mince (meat or plant based), brown it with 1 onion, then add 2-3 carrots, 1 bell pepper, ½ mug red lentils.

Then add 1 bottle of passata, and a little water to help get all the passata into the pot. Cook until cooked through.

Serve half of it as spaghetti bolognese on the first evening, and use the other half of the sauce as cottage pie topped with mashed potatoes.

Or trouble yourself to make white sauce (25g / 1oz butter, 25g / 1oz flour, ½ ltr / 17.5 fl oz milk, cook all together) and make lasagne instead.

(You know; stack mince, white sauce, lasagne sheet, white sauce, lasagne sheet and so on, until all is used up, then chuck cheese on top.)

Bake until it looks cooked.

Pil Pil King Prawns

– Sean Hedges-Quinn

<u>Ingredients</u>

225g / 8oz fresh peeled tiger prawns
1 onion finely chopped
2 garlic cloves finely chopped
2 tbs white wine
1 small chilli chopped
250g / 9oz tomato based pasta sauce
2 tsp runny honey
1 tsp smoked paprika
1 tbs chopped fresh chives
Salt and freshly ground black pepper

<u>Method</u>

Rinse the prawns and drain well.

Pre-heat a non-stick pan and dry fry the onion and garlic until soft.

Add the wine and the remaining ingredients, mixing well, and bring the sauce to the boil.

Just before you are ready to serve stir in the drained prawns and cook for 1-2 minutes.

Serve with rice and garnish with the chives.

BY Sean Hedges-Quinn x

Greek Prawn Saganaki
– Gloria Elmer

This is Gloria and Roger's favourite supper recipe, which we often have on a Saturday for supper. It can be prepared earlier in the day and once in the oven allows time for a nice glass of chilled wine.

Ingredients

1 onion chopped
1 or 2 cloves garlic
1 large tin chopped tomatoes
¼ tsp ground cayenne pepper
1 tsp smoked paprika
¼ tsp ground cumin
Large bag raw king prawns (thawed if frozen)
100g / 3½oz feta cheese
100g / 3½oz mature cheddar cheese, grated

Method

Gently fry the onion until soft, add the garlic, then add the chopped tomatoes and spices. Reduce until the mixture has thickened a little.

Arrange the raw prawns in two oven proof dishes, crumble the feta onto the prawns. Divide the tomato mixture into two and pour over the prawns and feta. Sprinkle the grated cheese over the tomato mixture.

Place in the oven on the middle shelf, Gas Mark 5 / 190°C and cook for 30 minutes.

Turn the oven off and allow to cool a bit before serving.

Serve with French bread, or other bread of your choice.

Wine that gladdens human hearts, oil to make their faces shine, and bread that sustains their hearts.

PSALM 104:15

Slow Cooker Sausage Casserole
- The Rev'd Lawrence Carey

As seen on TV! If you are not keen on soft pale sausages, you may want to brown them in a frying pan first.

<u>Ingredients</u>

10 sausages
1 large onion (diced)
1 pepper (sliced into 1cm pieces)
1 medium (400g / 14oz) sweet potato
2 tins chopped tomatoes
1 tbsp tomato puree
2 stock cubes (mixed with 500ml boiling water)
Salt & pepper to taste
Mixed herbs

<u>Method</u>

Cut each sausage into 4 or 5 pieces.

Slice/dice veg and add all the ingredients to the slow cooker.

Turn slow cooker on to low for 8 hours, until veg soft.

After 7 hours check it, and if you want the sauce thicker then add cornflour paste (cornflour and cold water) to the slow cooker and leave on for another hour.

Serve with potatoes or pasta, or chunky bread.

Sausage And Pasta Ragu
– Emma Knight

Great cheap and easy midweek dinner which everyone enjoys.

<u>Ingredients</u>

3 sausages
1 onion
½ cube frozen garlic
½ teaspoon chilli flakes
1 tin of tomatoes
½ table spoon balsamic vinegar
1 tablespoon of tomato puree
1 chicken stock cube
Sprinkle of fresh or dried basil
400g / 14oz pasta

<u>Method</u>

Chop the onion and add to a frying pan with a drizzle of oil and the garlic. Gently fry until soft. Remove the sausages from their skins and add to onions break them up into small pieces with a wooden spoon. Cook for 5 minutes until the sausages begin to colour.

Add the chicken stock cube, tomato puree, balsamic vinegar and 150ml of boiling water in a measuring jug and mix together. Set aside until the sausages are beginning to turn brown.

Once the sausages are starting to colour, add the chilli flakes, tinned tomatoes, basil and the chick stock. Cook for 15 minutes until it thickens.

Cook pasta and add to the ragu mixture and serve.

Sausage Plait
– Carole Groom

This may seem a little complicated at first but when you have made it once you will see it really is a quick and easy plait to make. It can be made earlier and put in the fridge. Brush with egg etc when ready to bake. Enjoy!

<u>Ingredients</u>

250g / 9oz JusRol puff pastry
1 lb / 453g sausagemeat or skinned sausages
Thin sliced shallots or small onions, to your taste
Small beaten egg
Sesame seeds (optional)

<u>Method</u>

On a floured board roll out the pastry to approximately 9" wide and 14" long.

Lightly mark it into thirds lengthways (do not cut through pastry).

Layer the onions down the centre third, leaving a small space top and bottom to seal.

Place the sausage meat over the onions and press down with fork.

Starting at the top on the right handside, cut the pastry through, making a triangle shape just up to the filling.

Then working down the right hand side cut through pastry strips of approx 1" wide all the way down, making another triangle at the bottom.

Repeat down the left hand side, reversing the triangle. These four triangles are used to seal top and bottom.

Starting at the top right, fold the triangle over the top of the sausagemeat to seal, then the left triangle. Now fold the right strips and the left strips alternatively, sealing the triangles over at the bottom to form the plait. It doesn't matter if some sausagemeat shows through, it all adds to the final appearance.

Brush with beaten egg.

Sprinkle with sesame seeds if required.

Place on lined baking sheet and bake on the top shelf of a hot oven. Fan 180°, 400°F, Gas 6 for approximately 40-45 minutes.

Serving options:

2 portions of salmon (400g / 14oz approx) served with tartare sauce.

Sweet mincemeat/sliced apple, sprinkling top with Demerara sugar and serving with hot custard or cream.

Croissant Wreath
– Karen Macfadyen

<u>Ingredients</u>

2 packets (240g / 8½oz) of chilled ready-made croissant dough

Mediterranean vegetable filling:
½ red pepper, chopped and de-seeded
2 spring onions, thinly sliced
85g / 3oz baby spinach leaves, thinly sliced
35g / 1½ oz black olives, sliced
55g / 2oz feta cheese, crumbled
115g / 4oz mozzarella cheese, grated
1 clove garlic, pressed
Zest and 1 tbsp juice from fresh lemon
2 tbsp mayonnaise

Chicken and broccoli filling:
225g / 8oz cooked chopped chicken
½ red pepper, de-seeded and chopped
4 broccoli florets, chopped (microwave first to soften)
1 clove garlic, pressed
115 / 4oz emmental, gruyere or mozzarella cheese, grated
2 tbsp mayonnaise

<u>Method</u>

Unroll the croissant dough, separate the 12 triangles.

Arrange the triangles in a circle, on a large greased baking sheet, with the wide ends of the triangles overlapping in the centre and the pointed end towards the outside. Leave approx 5" gap in the centre of the circle. Gently press together the edges of the triangles where they overlap to seal.

Mix the chosen filling together in a bowl.

Spoon the filling to form an even band around the circle, about

1" inside the widest end of the triangles. Bring the points of each triangle up over the filling and tuck the point under the wide end in the middle of the ring – creating a wreath with the filling totally covered.

Brush with milk or egg before baking for 25-30 minutes until deep golden brown.

Rachel's Happy Stew
– The Rev'd Rachel Revely

Based on a real story of transporting stew from Scunthorpe to Cambridge for the Cambridge Churches Homeless Project.

Once upon a time, on a cold December day with a biting frost, there was... a classic beef stew. The stew was very young but it knew it had already had a more exciting life than most baby stews, for it was on a journey, out of the kitchen, out into the big wide world.

Its pot had been sealed and bundled into a case, a bit like a suitcase but a 'stewcase', ready for its adventure. "Where am I going?" it pondered whilst the stew case rattled and scorched on gravel. But from the top of its gravy to the tips of its carrots, the stew was thrilled to be going on an adventure.

"Maybe I'm going to a high class restaurant where I'll be renamed casserole de boeuf a l'anglaise. Ooo, wouldn't that be fancy," the stew pondered.

Countless possibilities entered its comestible mind. "Maybe I am going to a school, a lunch club, or maybe I am going to a little cottage by the sea, where a poor fisherman's wife is going to serve me up to her husband who can't stand the smell of fish. Fish are very smelly; I'm glad I'm not a fish stew."

Anyway, the stew hoped that whoever ate it up would be full and happy, which is a funny thing to hope for, as I don't imagine that you or I would think very kindly about someone who was going to eat us up! But the stew was very kind, probably because it had been made out of good stock.

As the journey continued the stew realised it was travelling oh so far... "Why am I so important?" it thought to itself. "I am only a young stew after all. I am not very rich. I am not very wise. I cannot even bring lamb."

It wasn't sure why, but even stews knew that lambs were very important at this time of year. But oxen sometimes turned up too, and even donkeys. Although the stew was quite sure it didn't have any donkey in it. Nor any horse. "Only the best beef shin from a very high class butcher," it thought with a little bit of pride.

With a clatter and a thump the stew stopped moving. "This is it!" it thought to itself, getting more and more excited. "I cannot wait to see where I am." The stew was quickly lifted and it felt the wheels of case hit the ground. It was on the move again - tilting and sloshing, to and fro, up and down.

The stew heard lots of feet walking, trotting and even running as people clearly wanted to get somewhere very quickly! It had to be somewhere important.

A thought struck the stew which made its onions quiver. Maybe it was going to London to be lunch for someone special! "Where will this journey end?"

The stew strained to hear (and all the best stews are strained to stop them being lumpy and grumpy.) Right on cue, there was an announcement: "This train calls at Peterborough... Ely... Cambridge... London." The stew bubbled with excitement. They really *were* going to London. "Maybe I'll end up on the plate of the Prime Minister. Maybe even the King!"

The journey continued on the stew could feel the excitement mounting in is turnips. "I can meet so many important people," it thought to itself. "I can see Heads of State, royalty, celebrities, leaders."

The stew felt the train slow down... Surely it couldn't be London already? Maybe it wasn't going to be a royal stew after all.

The next station was Cambridge. And the stew grew even more proud. "What if I am dinner for some of the cleverest people in the world? People who write about science, art and history." The stew thought how thrilling it would be to be the sustaining cuisine to some great think tank. "Maybe I will see the inside of a great hall, or a candle lit formal meal." The stew daydreamed about all the silver cutlery laid out and bubbled in anticipation.

The stew could hear the streets of Cambridge, the hustle and bustle of the train station, the last minute shoppers racing through the streets, a man shouting "ho ho ho", the bells of bicycles ringing out amidst the hubbub. Suddenly the noise faded and the stew thought it could nearly hear the stars twinkling in the night sky. When out of the silence came a lone voice singing a beautiful melody, *"Once in royal David's city, stood a lowly cattle shed"*...

"It's Christmas Eve!" thought the stew. "Perhaps I am going to meet Santa Claus or be Christmas lunch."

Suddenly the carols were becoming quieter, there were fewer people and not as many bicycle bells punctuating the hurly-burly. "Surely, I'm not going to an ordinary place? I am a special stew and need to be eaten by special people!"

The journey ended, the stewcase was opened, and the stew discovered, much to its surprise, it was in a church!

"Maybe I am going to be eaten by the Archbishop of Canterbury ... that would make me very important after all."

The stew was placed on a hob and heated up again; it bubbled and bubbled until finally it was placed on a table. It waited for a king, or a professor, or an archbishop to tuck in. But it noticed, to its horror, there wasn't even shiny silver cutlery, not even matching plates!

What was happening? Suddenly a whole load of very ordinary looking people were gathering around the stew. In fact, on closer inspection, they were more than ordinary - their clothes were torn, their beards were long and ragged, they were wearing lots of coats on top of each other, some of them had gloves with holes.

"These people are not important, not special, not royalty." The stew tried to say "No! I'm not for the likes of you!" But being a stew, no words came out.

It was no good. The stew was being eaten up by all those people - who were cold, tired and very hungry.

But the strangest thing began to happen... The stew (the bit that was left, at least) realised those people weren't cold, tired and hungry any more. They seemed content, filled, and maybe even happier. The stew heard the night go on - there was laughter, games, fun and friendship. Love!

"This was why I was made," the stew thought to itself... "not to feed people who were already full, not to warm people already warm. This was the reason I was brought such a long way - not to impress clever people or to show off to important people, but to show love to the people who needed it most." The stew realised it had been made, journeyed and eaten with love.

"Is there any more of that delicious stew?" it heard echoing around the church. It beamed with pride and thought, "Yes, this is why I am here."

The last spoonful of stew had been licked clean. Back in the chapel the carols had finished. The night was silent and dark. But in the hearts of the people who had eaten and heard, there was a new recipe. Even better than a classic beef stew. It was a recipe for a new world. And it started not in a stew case, but in a manger.

This easy slow cooker beef stew recipe is filled with savoury flavors, hearty potatoes and veggies to make it filling and delicious.

Ingredients

750g / 26½oz beef - it doesn't have to be shin, any beef will do.
2 large onions
1 ltr beef stock
250ml red wine (not essential)
1 tsp sugar
1 tbsp tomato puree
1 tbsp Worcestershire sauce
1 tsp balsamic vinegar
2 cloves of garlic
Thyme
Vegetables - any you like but my traditional choices are carrots, potatoes, and turnip; peas also work well

Method

Turn on the slow cooker in the morning.

Season the beef with salt, pepper and thyme.

Fry onions and garlic in butter and add sugar until brown, stirring regularly as the sugar could burn.

Add the beef and sear.

Add the balsamic vinegar, Worcestershire sauce and tomato puree, and stir.

Add the red wine and the beef stock.

Add the vegetables of your choice and top up with water if needed.

Leave in the slow cooker all day and eat for a scrumptious dinner.

Cabbage And Bacon Stir Fry
- Mona Taylor

<u>Ingredients</u>

500g / 17½oz firm cabbage (sliced thinly and washed)
2 onions/ leeks (sliced thinly and washed)
250g / 9oz bacon (cut into strips)
1-2tbsps olive oil
1 tsp chinese five spice

<u>Method</u>

Heat the oil in a wide pan.

Sprinkle in the spice and fry for 30 seconds.

Add the bacon and stir fry for 2-3 mins to seal the meat.

Add the onions/leeks and stir fry for 2-3 mins.

Lastly add the cabbage and stir fry for 2-3 mins.

Serves 4.

Pork And Apple Casserole
- The Rev'd Lawrence Carey

As seen on TV! This could be served with pasta or potatoes and vegetables, to your taste.

<u>Ingredients</u>

1 onion (diced)
4 apples (peeled, cored and diced)
Pork (diced)
1 litre apple juice
Soy sauce
300 ml single cream

<u>Method</u>

Add diced onion, diced apple and diced pork along with the litre of apple juice and soy sauce into the slow cooker together.

Stir and turn slow cooker on low for 8 hours.

Add cream and leave for another ½ hour.

If the 'sauce' is too runny for your taste, then thicken with 1- 2 tbsp cornflour and water paste mixture and leave on for another ½ hour.

Steak And Kidney Pudding
- Caroline Fisk

This is a dish that I use on a Sunday; I prepare everything before church, put it on, and it's ready and waiting for Sunday dinner.

<u>Ingredients</u>

185g / 6oz self raising flour
85g / 3oz shredded suet
Pinch of salt
450g / 1lb lean stewing steak, cut into cubes
225g / 8oz ox or lamb kidney, cut into cubes
1 medium onion, finely chopped
Black pepper

<u>Method</u>

Preheat the slow cooker on high.

Grease a litre pudding bowl.

Mix together the flour, suet and seasoning. Add enough water to make a dough. Roll out two thirds of the dough onto a lightly floured surface and line the pudding basin. Reserve the remaining third for the lid.

Mix together the steak, kidney, onion, salt and pepper and place into the pastry shell. Add 2 tbsp water.

Roll out the reserved pastry. Moisten the edges of the pastry shell and press the lid into position.

Lightly grease foil or greaseproof paper and cover the pudding. Fold a length of foil/paper to leave under the bowl with the ends loose in order to place and remove the bowl in and out of the slow cooker.

Place the bowl in the slow cooker and pour in enough boiling water to come halfway up the side of the bowl. Replace the lid of the slow cooker, cook on high for 6-8. DO NOT SNEAK A LOOK!

Remove the bowl, using the foil/paper handle. Remove the greaseproof paper/foil from the pudding and turn out onto a plate. Serve with your choice of vegetables.

Chicken Simla (For 4)
– Marilyn Smith

Ingredients

4 boneless chicken breasts
1 rounded tbs flour
1 large onion
65g / 2½oz butter
1 rounded tbs curry powder
400ml / ¾ pint chicken stock
⅛ level teaspoon cayenne
¼ level teaspoon ginger
¼ level teaspoon salt
Black pepper
2 level tbs mango chutney, chopped
15g / 1oz sultanas
8 oz / 226g wholemeal pasta rings
150ml / 5 fl oz soured cream
Paprika

Method

Skin chicken, lay flat on a board, cut into strips 1/2" thick and toss in flour.

Finely chop onion.

Melt 50g / 1¾oz butter in a large saucepan, add onion and fry over a low heat until tender.

Stir in curry powder and cook for a further minute. Add floured chicken and fry until pale golden brown.

Stir in stock, cayenne pepper, ground ginger, salt and black pepper.

Bring to the boil, stirring.

Add chutney and sultanas. Simmer, cover for around half an hour, stirring occasionally, until tender.

Cook pasta rings in plenty of boiling salted water for 10-15 minutes, or until tender. Drain.

Return to the pan with remaining 15g / ½oz butter. Toss over a medium heat. Pour into a dish.

Add soured cream to chicken. Stir until evenly mixed.

Taste and adjust seasoning to liking.

Serve chicken with the pasta rings, sprinkled with paprika.

Easy Chicken Curry
– Emma Knight

A great alternative to a take away and healthier too! Serves 4.

Ingredients

2 large chicken breasts
2 onions grated
1 cube frozen garlic
1 cube frozen ginger
1 cube frozen chillies
1 tin chopped tomatoes
1 tin coconut milk
1 tablespoon mango chutney
2 tablespoons Pataks Tikka Masala paste

Method

In a frying pan sweat down the onions in a tablespoon of oil with the garlic, ginger and chillies.

Once the onions are soft add 1 tablespoon of paste and mango chutney. Add the tinned tomatoes and coconut milk (you may not need all of the water depending on how runny you like it).

In a dish add the other tablespoon of paste to the chicken and cover.

Add a tablespoon of oil to another frying pan and add the chicken breasts whole. Cook for around 10 minutes on each side, remove and cut up on a chopping board. They will probably still be pink inside, that's okay.

Add them to the sauce and cook for another 15 minutes or until chicken is cooked all the way through.

Serve with rice and naan bread!

So whether you eat or drink or whatever you do, do it all for the glory of God.

1 CORINTHIANS 10:31

Slow Cooker Chicken Stew
- Martin Carter

Slow Cooker Chicken Stew is a simple dump and go recipe that is both tangy and delicious. Great for busy people who need a nutritious, family friendly, one pot meal!

<u>Ingredients</u>

4 x chicken (breast or thigh)
2 x onions
3 x carrots
6 x potatoes
Frozen peas
1 x garlic clove
1 x tinned chopped tomatoes
6 x chestnut mushrooms
Tarragon
Tomato puree
Worcestershire or Tabasco sauce
Knob of butter
1 x vegetable stock

<u>Method</u>

Chop onions, mushrooms and potatoes in to chunky cubes.

Slice carrots and finely chop the garlic clove.

Place all the prepared vegetables (not the peas yet!) and garlic into the slow cooker, followed by the chicken, and add 1 tablespoon of sugar, tarragon, butter, salt and pepper to the pot.

Then add the tinned tomatoes, tomato puree, worcestershire sauce or Tabasco sauce and vegetable stock and give the pot a good stir.

Cook in the slow cooker on high for 5 – 6 hrs or low 7 – 8 hrs.

One hour before the end stir in the frozen peas.

Serve with crusty bread to take away the winter chill.

Chicken Pie
- Mona Taylor

<u>Ingredients</u>

500g / 17½oz puff pastry
50g / 1¾oz butter/ margarine
50g / 1¾oz flour
1tbsp olive oil
½pt chicken stock
2 chicken breasts, cubed
2 slices of bacon, chopped into cubes
50g / 1¾oz sweetcorn (tinned or frozen)
1 leek, washed and sliced
1 teaspoon freshly chopped herbs
Black pepper and salt to taste
Milk to glaze the pie

<u>Method</u>

Light the oven Gas 6/ 200°C.

Heat the oil in a pan on a medium heat.

Fry the bacon and leeks for 3/4 mins. Stir.

Add the cubed chicken and cook until browned; 5-10 mins.

Add the chicken stock and sweetcorn. Stir and turn down the heat to low.

Blend the flour and margarine/butter to form a paste in a small bowl.

Remove the chicken from the heat.

Add small pieces of the flour/butter paste to the chicken mixture. Stir each time until dissolved and thickened.

Stir in the chopped herbs and check the seasoning. Add black pepper and salt as needed.

Place in a pie dish.

Roll out pastry large enough to cover the top of the pie.

Cut off any excess pastry and save to make decorations.

Brush with milk. Pierce top with a fork.

Back on top shelf for 20-25 mins until golden brown.

Diet Cola Chicken
- Caren Elwis

This dish is so simple and a family favourite.

<u>Ingredients</u>
4 chicken breasts cut into bite-size chunks
One red, one yellow, one green pepper cut into bite-size chunks
One onion finely chopped
330 mils of Diet Cola
200 mils of hot chicken stock
8 tablespoons of Passata with onions and garlic
4 teaspoons of tomato purée
Two garlic cloves finely chopped
2 teaspoons of gluten-free Worcestershire sauce
1 tablespoon of dark soy sauce
1 teaspoon of mixed herbs
200g / 7oz of sugar snap peas

<u>Method</u>

Spray a large pan with cooking spray place over a high heat.

Add chicken peppers onion and stirfry for 5 to 7 minutes.

Add Cola, stock, Passata, tomato purée, garlic, Worcestershire sauce, soy sauce and herbs, stir well.

Bring to the boil and cover; reduce heat and simmer for 12 to 15 minutes.

Add the sugar snap peas, stir, and increase the heat for another 10 to 15 minutes or until chicken is cooked and veg is tender.

Sweet And Sour Chicken
- The Rev'd Lawrence Carey

<u>Ingredients</u>

4 boneless chicken breasts (cut into 1" pieces)
1 tin (398ml) pineapple chunks
1 red pepper (diced)
1 green pepper (diced)
1¼ cups sugar
¾ cup vinegar
½ cup ketchup
2 tbsp soy sauce
3 tbsp cornflour
1 tsp minced garlic
½ tsp minced ginger

<u>Method</u>

Add chicken, pineapple and peppers (all chopped/diced) into the Slow Cooker together.

Mix sugar, vinegar, ketchup, soy sauce, corn flour, garlic and ginger in a bowl.

Pour mixture over chicken etc in slow cooker and cook on low for 3 hours.

If the 'sauce' is too runny for your taste, then thicken with 1- 2 tbsp cornflour and water paste mixture and leave on for another ½ hour.

Serve over cooked rice or noodles.

Persian Chicken (Or Turkey)
- The Rev'd Canon Christopher Chapman

The ancient Persian people enjoyed cooking meat with fruit and the following recipe is derived from a traditional Persian meal.

I use this recipe quite often as it is a quick and easy way to use up leftovers, and equally good as a meal for a larger number of people, using chicken thighs or drumsticks, cooked, boned and diced then fried as described and cooked in a slow cooker.

Ingredients

2 large onions, sliced
2 cooking apples, roughly chopped
500g / 17½oz cooked chicken, diced
Juice of 1 lemon
1 tsp ground cinnamon
500ml Chicken stock
3 mushrooms, sliced
Handful of grapes, cut in half (or sultanas/raisins if preferred)
Salt and black pepper, to taste

Cooked chicken can be replaced with a cheaper cut of fresh chicken, but this will need to be cooked well before adding the other ingredients.

Method

Gently fry the onions in the oil until soft and golden. Add the chopped apple, mushrooms and grapes and cook until soft. Add the chicken stock and cooked meat. Stir and heat thoroughly, slowly adding the lemon juice, cinnamon, salt and pepper.

Once cooked, the meal can be kept warm in a slow cooker.

Serve with easy cook rice.

Slow Cooker Beef In Beer
- Martin Carter

Slow Cooker Beef In Beer is a simple dump and go recipe that is both tasty and warming. Great for busy people who need a nutritious, family friendly, one pot meal!

Ingredients

Diced beef (stewing steak, brisket, chuck steak)
Flour (Plain)
1 x can of Mackeson Stout
6 x shallots
6 x chestnut mushrooms
Rosemary (dried or fresh)
Tomato puree
Worcestershire or Tabasco Sauce
Knob of butter
1 x beef stock
1 x garlic bread baguette

Method

Brown stewing steak in a pan (for best results), brisket, chuck steak has lots of connective tissue which breaks down and renders the beef tender in the slow cooker).

Optionally, dust the browned off steak in the flour if wanting a slightly thicker gravy and set aside.

Quarter shallots, mushrooms and potatoes to chunky cubes, and finely chop the garlic.

Place all the prepared vegetables and garlic into the slow cooker, followed by the diced beef, then add sugar, rosemary, butter, salt and pepper to the pot.

Then add one can of Mackeson Stout, tomato puree, Worcestershire Sauce or Tabasco sauce and the beef stock, giving it a good stir.

Cook in the slow cooker on high for 5 – 6 hrs or low 7 – 8 hrs.

Serving suggestion: For that little extra feel good factor; 45 minutes before the end of cooking time, add slices of toasted garlic baguette on top of the beef in beer and continue cooking time.

Mock Goose
– Marilyn Smith

Ingredients

1lb / 453g pork sausages, skinned or 1lb / 453g sausage meat
1 onion
1lb / 453g mashed potato
Sage
Pepper and salt

Method

Break up the sausages with a fork and put alternative layers of sausage and potatoes, seasoned with chopped onion, sage, pepper and salt, into a fireproof dish.

Bake until brown and serve with apple sauce.

Eric's Surprisingly Simple Dinner Delight
- Eric Baker

<u>Ingredients</u>

Any ready-made meal from the frozen or chilled aisle of your local
supermarket
Money with which to buy the meal
One (1) plate
One (1) microwave
One (1) bottle of wine/beer

<u>Method</u>

Purchase the ready-made meal of your choice.

Follow the instructions on the packaging to prepare.

Drink enough that you won't notice the difference in taste. I do
always try to make sure I have some fresh vegetables to go with
the wine.

Enjoy!

Sweet Dishes

The Thomas Who Came To Tea

Easy Bake Cupcakes
– Margaret Bloomfield

The reason why I like to make these are they are easy and can be decorated lots of different ways. My favourite is the butterfly design with a chocolate button in the centre.

<u>Ingredients</u>

Cupcakes:
110g / 4oz butter or margarine, softened at room temperature
110g / 4oz caster sugar
2 eggs, lightly beaten
1 tsp vanilla extract
110g / 4oz self raising flour
1-2 tbs milk

Buttercream icing:
140g / 5oz softened butter
280g / 10oz icing sugar
1-2 tbs milk

<u>Method</u>

Preheat the oven to Fan 160°C Electric 180° Gas 4.

Line a 12 hole muffin tin with paper cases.

Cream the butter and sugar together until pale.

Beat in the eggs a little at a time. Stir in the vanilla extract.

Fold in the flour using a large metal spoon, adding a little milk until the mixture is of a dropping consistency.

Spoon the mixture into the paper cases until they are half full.

Bake in the oven for 10-15 minutes until golden brown on top and a skewer into one of the cakes comes out clean.

Set aside for 10 minutes and remove from the tin and cool on a wire rack.

For the icing:

Beat the butter in a large bowl until soft. Add half the icing sugar and beat until smooth.

Add the remaining icing sugar with 1 tbsp of the milk adding more milk as necessary until the mixture is smooth and creamy.

Once the cupcakes are cooled smooth on the icing as you choose.

Chocolate Chip Muffins
- Edith Abbott

<u>Ingredients</u>

250g / 9oz plain flour
100g / 3½oz sugar
3 tsp baking powder
½ tsp salt
175ml milk
75ml vegetable oil
1 egg
125g / 4½oz chocolate chips

Topping:
3 tbs caster sugar
2 tbs brown sugar

<u>Method</u>

Mix together the flour, sugar, baking powder, salt and chocolate chips.

In a small bowl mix the oil, milk and egg.

Add together, mix well and put in muffin cases. Sprinkle tops with caster and brown sugar.

Bake at 200°C for 20-25 minutes. Makes 12 muffins.

Sponge Cake
– The Rev'd Cat Connelly

This is my favourite sponge cake recipe as it is so easy! It makes a very light and delicate cake. It makes good cupcakes too - this amount will make 24 cupcakes. Cook for 18-20 minutes.

Ingredients

6oz / 170g plain flour
6oz / 170g caster sugar
6oz / 170g margarine or softened butter
3 tsp baking powder
3 eggs

Method

Chuck everything all together in a big bowl and mix well for a couple of minutes until the batter is light and creamy.

Divide evenly between the two tins.

Cook for 20-25 minutes until the cakes spring back when pressed lightly in the middle.

Cover with a tea towel and cool in tins. Once cooled, remove from tins and sandwich together with your choice of filling (seedless raspberry jam is great!).

You can substitute 1oz of flour for cocoa powder, and do half and half caster with soft brown sugar for a chocolate version.

Fruit Cake (Suitable For Diabetics)
– Val Derrett

Ingredients

¼ pint sunflower oil
7oz / 198g raisins
7oz / 198g sultanas
5oz / 142g pitted dates
¼ pint skimmed milk
9oz / 255g self raising flour
1 tsp mixed spice
3 eggs
½ tsp bicarbonate of soda

Method

Cut dates into smaller pieces.

Put all dry ingredients in bowl and mix together.

Then add milk, beaten eggs and sunflower oil and mix well.

Grease cake tin before turning into it.

Cook on gas 2 / 150°C for two hours.

Aunt Paola's Caprese (Almond And Chocolate) Cake
- The Rev'd Simone Ramacci

A staple of our New Year lunch back home, my great-aunt Paola makes this and the walnut cake every year. Sometimes I also had these as birthday cakes.

Ingredients

6 eggs
250g / 9oz almond flour
250g / 9oz dark chocolate
250g / 9oz sugar
250g / 9oz butter

Method

Mix the butter with the sugar using a spatula until soft and mousse-like, then add egg yolks one by one, ensuring each is thoroughly mixed in before adding the next.

Melt the dark chocolate in a bain-marie, taking care to stir throughout, and add to your mixture, followed by the flour, and finally whip the egg whites and add. Mix thoroughly after each step.

Coat a cake tin with butter and flour, and bake for roughly 1h20m at 180°C / Gas 4. Use a knife or baking stick to check if baked.

Easy Lemon Cheesecake
– Emma Knight

<u>Ingredients</u>

300g / 10½oz digestive biscuits
150g / 5¼oz butter or margarine
1 Tub of soft cheese
1 300ml carton of double cream
1 lemon
50g / 1¾oz caster sugar

<u>Method</u>

Melt the butter in a saucepan. Crush the digestive biscuits in a bowl with a rolling pin.

Add the digestives to the melted butter and mix well. Push the mixture into an 8 inch cake tin and place in the fridge.

Beat the double cream until very thick. Beat the cheese in a separate bowl until softened. Grate the lemon rind into the cheese, then fold the double cream gently into the cheese.

Juice the lemon and add to the mixture with the sugar.

Place on top of the biscuit base and leave to set – optional decorate with strawberrries or other fruit.

To mix it up replace the lemon with 3 crushed up crunchies for a crunchie cheesecake!

Delicious, Easy German Apple Cake
– The Rev'd Canon Jutta Brueck

Ingredients

100-125 g / 4oz butter
100g / 3-4 oz sugar (*How sweet do you like your cakes?*)
3 eggs
Pinch of salt
Juice of half a lemon (or 2-3 drops of lemon flavouring)
200g / 8oz flour
2 teaspoons of baking powder (*I prefer plain flour+baking powder to self-raising flour*)
1-4 tablespoons of milk (*if the mixture is very firm; it wants to be quite firm!*)
500-750g / 17½-26½oz apples, peeled, core removed, quartered, with two or three cuts on the top. (*You can stop the apples from turning brown by putting some lemon juice on*).

Method

Mix the **butter** and **sugar**, and then whisk the **eggs** into the mixture until it's very smooth. Add the **salt** when you put the eggs in, and the **lemon** half way through the whisking process. (*It's best to use an electrical or mechanical mixer.*)

Sieve the flour and baking powder, and slowly stir it into the mixture with a wooden spoon. Add the **milk** if necessary.

Grease a baking tin (~10 inches, round, ideally a 'springform'), and put the dough mixture in. Arrange the apple pieces in circles.

Preheat the oven to **180° Celsius / Gas 4**; bake **for 40 – 50 minutes**.

When it's cooled down, sprinkle on some icing sugar. (do it through a sieve then you will have no lumps.)

Enjoy, just as it is, or with some crème fraiche. Guten Appetit.

Gran Clelia's Chocolate And Pears Cake
- The Rev'd Simone Ramacci

My gran usually bakes this as a moreish breakfast option when we visit during the summer. The pears help keeping the cake extra moist. The original recipe (without pears) is from a 1940s Italian cook book.

Ingredients

200g / 7oz flour
250g / 9oz sugar
100g / 3½oz unsweetened cocoa
Peel of one orange
A pinch (2 grams) of cinnamon
4 grams of baking soda
4 grams of cream of tartar (can be replaced with baking powder)
250 ml of whole milk
Pears

Method

Add together the dry ingredients, taking care to sift the flour. Mix with the milk until silky smooth.

Butter a cake tin (preferably a ring shaped one) and gently dust with breadcrumbs. Fill with your cake batter and scatter thin pear slices or chunks according to taste.

Bake until cooked.

Lemon Drizzle Cake
– Sylvia Dickerson

Ingredients

4oz / 113g margarine
6oz / 170g sugar
6oz / 170g flour
4 tbsp milk
2 eggs
1 lemon
3 rounded tbsp icing sugar

Method

Cream margarine and sugar. Beat in eggs and flour, grated lemon rind and milk.

Cook for 40-45 minutes at 180 C.

Mix icing sugar and lemon juice and pour over the cake when removed from the oven.

Housekeepers Cake
– Caroline Fisk

This is a recipe I was given at school in 1972-3 and has been a popular favourite since then. When Daniel was at primary school he came home one day asking me to make our special Housekeepers Cake for a cake competition at school the next day. So the evening was spent duly baking. I took it in with him in the morning, only to be told by an astounded teacher that there WAS no competition. Apparently, Daniel simply fancied taking in a cake!

Ingredients

6oz / 170g sr flour
3oz / 85g marge
3oz / 85g granulated sugar
1 egg
½ tsp mixed spice
3oz / 85g currants/sultanas
Milk to mix

You can add extra fruit or mixed spice as per your taste.

Method

Rub fat into flour.

Add sugar and currants.

Beat eggs and stir into mixture, add milk. This makes a fairly stiff mixture. Place into loaf tin.

Sprinkle top of cake with sugar and bake in the oven at ¾ hour / Gas Mark 4 / 350°F and whatever the equivalent not 1970s temperatures are!

Best eaten with lots of tea.

Elijah looked, and there at his head was a cake baked on hot stones, and a jar of water. He ate and drank, and lay down again.

1 KINGS 19:6

Aunt Paola's Walnut Cake
- The Rev'd Simone Ramacci

Ingredients:

6 eggs
250g / 9oz of walnut flour
250g / 9oz of sugar

Method

Whip together the yolks and the sugar. Mix in your flour, and then add whipped egg whites. Mix thoroughly.

Coat a cake tin with butter and flour, and bake for roughly 1h20m at 180°C / Gas 4. Use a knife or baking stick to check if baked.

Fruit Shortcakes
- Lyanne Brendt

Ingredients

8oz / 226g self raising flour
4oz / 113g margarine
4oz / 113g granulated sugar
Mixed dried fruit
Milk to mix

Method

Cut and rub in the flour and fat until it resembles fine breadcrumbs. Stir in sugar and dried fruit. Carefully add milk and pull together with hands until dry ingredients are absorbed but not too wet. Press out on lightly floured board and shape into a square or rectangle about ¾ inch or 2cm deep. Cut into squares or oblongs. Makes about 10.

Space out on a lined baking tray, sprinkle a little sugar on top and bake in a pre-heated oven at 200°C for about 15 minutes until golden brown.

Marble Cake
– Andrea McDonald

<u>Ingredients</u>

200g / 7oz self raising flour
50g / 1¾oz cornflour (it helps make the cake fluffy)
3-4 eggs
175g / 6¼oz sugar
175g / 6¼oz butter

<u>Method</u>

Start with the wet ingredients and the sugar, then add the flour.

Divide the dough by pouring half of it in a loaf tin.

To the remaining add 4 tbsp cocoa powder and 3 tbsp sugar.

Pour on top then use a skewer to go round the tin in a circle.

Bake for 40 mins on 160°C / Gas 3.

Enjoy the pattern when slicing it.

Myrtle's Mighty Celebration Cake
– Myrtle Hughes

Ingredients

3lb / 1.36kg sugar
2lb / 907g self raising flour
1lb / 453g butter
Vanilla essence
Nutmeg
Brandy
1lb / 453g fruit

Method

Mix together. Cook in round tin.

Edward's Best Mince Pies
- The Rev'd Edward Pritchett

Ingredients

For the pastry:
375g / 13oz plain flour
250g / 9oz butter, softened
250g / 9oz caster sugar, plus extra for sprinkling
1 medium egg

For the filling:
2 x 400g / 14oz jars mincemeat

Optional extras:
2 tangerines, zest grated and flesh chopped
1 apple, finely diced

Method

Preheat the oven to 200°C / 400°F / Gas 6.

To make the pastry, rub the flour, butter, sugar and egg together with a dash of cold water until it just comes together as a dough. Wrap the pastry in cling film and set aside to chill in the fridge.

Add apple and tangerine to mincemeat if desired.

Roll out the pastry to a 3mm / ⅛th" thickness. With a round pastry cutter, cut out discs of pastry. Press the pastry into the muffin cups and fill each one so that it reaches three-quarters of the way up the side of the pastry-lined cup.

Cut out lids to the mince pies using either circular or star cutter. Place a lid on top of each pie and gently push down. Sprinkle with caster sugar.

Bake for 20 minutes, then transfer to a wire rack to cool. Dust with icing sugar and serve warm, maybe with a helping of cream.

Cheats Tiramisu
– Karen Macfadyen

This can be made into individual dishes but I think it's nicer made in a larger dish and shared. A colleague gave me this recipe over 20 years ago and is regularly used. Enjoy.

<u>Ingredients</u>

2 tbsp instant coffee
2 tbsp caster sugar
3 tbsp brandy or rum
8 trifle sponges, cut into thick fingers
8oz / 226g pot mascarpone cheese
¼ pt double cream
½ pt ready to serve custard
2oz / 57g plain chocolate, grated
2 tsp cocoa powder, sifted

<u>Method</u>

Place the coffee and sugar in a measuring jug. Add 3 tbsp (45ml) boiling water and stir until the coffee and sugar are dissolved. Add the brandy or rum and top up with cold water to make 8fl oz (250ml) of liquid.

Place half the sponges in a shallow serving dish. Slowly pour over half the coffee liquid.

Place the mascarpone cheese, double cream and custard into a bowl and whip until soft, smooth and creamy. Spread half the mixture over the soaked sponges and sprinkle with half the chocolate.

Add the remaining sponges and slowly pour over the remaining coffee liquid until fully soaked.

Spread over the remaining mascarpone mixture and sprinkle with the remaining chocolate and the cocoa powder.

Can be served immediately, but is better slightly chilled until
required.

Gran Clelia's Custard Tiramisu
- The Rev'd Simone Ramacci

Another summer favourite, this family twist on an Italian classic does away with the heavier mascarpone cheese, and is more child friendly by replacing coffee with cocoa. You can add strawberries or raspberries on top if you'd like. The custard recipe comes from a 19c cookbook.

Ingredients

1 litre of milk
200g / 7oz sugar
8 egg yolks
Vanilla pods
Savoiardi (sponge finger) biscuits
Unsweetened cocoa powder

Method

For the custard: mix together the egg yolks and sugar in a saucepan. On the hob, add the milk in slowly, steer thoroughly but delicately until cooked. If you see vapour coming out of the pan, you should lower the heat or you'll end up with scrambled eggs. Add the vanilla pods to taste towards the end. It will be ready when it is quite thick and clings to a wooden spoon.

Alternatively, you can replace the custard above with your go-to crème pat recipe.

Assembly: layer a flat-bottom container with the biscuits, and drizzle with cocoa powder dissolved in hot water, taking care not to soak them so much that they fall apart. Cover with a layer of custard, and keep alternating moistened biscuits and custard until you run out. Custard should be the top layer.

Sprinkle cocoa powder on top, and put in the fridge to set.

It is not good to eat too much honey, nor is it honorable to search out matters that are too deep.

PROVERBS 25:27

Banana Ice Cream (Vegan)
– Lyanne Brendt

I've used raspberries instead of the cocoa and peanut butter, and that's delicious! This was the first time I made it, and my taste testers were Rob and his friend Peter. Peter said it was delicious and asked for the recipe for his mum. Rob asked why I'd spoiled raspberry ice cream by adding bananas...

Use those bananas you got from the top up shop!

You need some sort of blender. Mine came with my food processor. You could use a stick blender, I'm sure.

4 really ripe bananas. Peel, break into short pieces, put in a freezer safe container (that ice cream tub you washed out and put in the cupboard is perfect!) and freeze. They need at least an hour, but you can leave them there for as long as you want. And if you've got more bananas to use up, put lots in the freezer. But in tubs of 4 at a time, to make it easier for you when you go to use them.

When you're ready to make the ice cream, take a tub of prepped banana pieces from the freezer and leave them on the side while you get the food processor & other ingredients ready. This will let them soften just a little, and be easier to blend.

My other ingredients are 2 teaspoons of cocoa & 1 tablespoon of crunchy peanut butter.

Blend the bananas. At first, they will rattle around the food processor alarmingly! Then they will begin to grind down, and then become a smooth puree. Stop the blender every so often to scrape them down the sides and check it's not over heating.

When the banana has become a smooth pale puree, add your flavourings! And blend a bit more to combine. Then serve delicious vegan ice cream! It does keep in the freezer once made, unless your son knows it's there...

Any soft fruit you have laying around would be good. Apple and blackberry would be lovely.

Sticky Toffee Pudding
- Mona Taylor

<u>Ingredients</u>

120g / 4¼oz dates, chopped
200 mls water
1 teabag
Pinch bicarbonate of soda
35g / 1¼oz butter
120g / 4¼oz caster sugar
1 large egg, beaten
120g / 4¼oz SR flour
1/2 tsp vanilla essence

Sauce:
25g / 1oz butter
1tbsp golden syrup
120g / 4¼oz soft brown sugar
3 tsps single cream

<u>Method</u>

Heat the oven 180°C/ Gas 4.

Grease an ovenproof dish

Put the dates, water and teabag into a small saucepan and simmer for 5mins.

Remove the teabag. Add the bicarbonate of soda.

Beat the butter and sugar until creamy.

Add the egg and beat well.

Stir in the flour and date mixture and vanilla essence. Mix thoroughly.

Pour into the prepared tin.

Bake for 30mins until firm to the touch.

For the sauce: put the sugar, syrup and butter into a small saucepan. Bring to the boil and boil for 1-2 mins.

Remove from the heat and add the cream.

Pour over the pudding.

Marmalade Bread And Butter Pudding
– Karen Macfadyen

<u>Ingredients</u>

2 rounded tbsp dark chunky orange marmalade
1oz / 25g candied peel, finely chopped, or a handful of raisins
6 slices white bread, ½"/1cm thicky, with crusts left on
2oz / 50g softened butter
10 fl oz / 275ml whole milk
2½ fl oz / 60ml double cream
3 large eggs
3 oz / 75g sugar
Grated zest of 1 large orange
1 level tbsp Demerara sugar

<u>Method</u>

Preheat the oven to Gas 4 / 350°F / 180°C.

Lightly grease a baking dish 7x9x2" (18x23x5cm).

Generously butter the slices of bread on one side, then spread the marmalade on 3 of these slices. Put the other 3 slices on top (buttered side down) as in a sandwich.

Spread some butter over the top slice of each sandwich and cut each one into quarters to make triangles or squares. Arrange the sandwich pieces, butter side up, overlapping each other into the baking dish, standing almost upright.

Whisk the milk, cream, eggs and sugar together and pour this over the bread.

Scatter on the grated orange zest, Demerara sugar, candied peel or raisins. Place on a high shelf and bake for 35-40 minutes until puffy and golden and the top crust is crunchy.

Serve whilst hot with either crème fraîche or pouring cream.

Other varieties you could try:
Chocolate chunks
Soft fruit such as raspberries or blueberries with lemon curd or white chocolate
Poached rhubarb and pecans

Gingerbread Men
– Lyanne Brendt

It's time to get ready for All Age All Saints service, and the supermarkets haven't got big gingerbread people in for the young people to decorate into gingerbread saints! Don't panic, just use this delicious and simple recipe adapted from BBC Good Food. Experimentation is required for gluten free gingerbread, and savoury saints.

My cutters include stereotypical gingerbread man and gingerbread lady, and ninjabread people (and a little gingerbread person, but that was too small, so stayed in the box with the gruffalo and storm trooper).

Be joined by extended youth group - youth group with Younger siblings and cousins and parents, and other people who want to decorate them - and have a wonderful time! Who's your favourite saint?

Ingredients

700g / 24½oz plain flour, plus extra for rolling out
2 tsp bicarbonate of soda
4 tsp ground ginger
2 tsp ground cinnamon
250g / 9oz unsalted dairy free Flora
350g / 12¼oz light soft brown sugar
2 free-range eggs, or your preferred egg replacer (I use organ powdered egg replacer as it has a long shelf life)
8 tbsp golden syrup

Method

Sift together the flour, the bicarbonate of soda, and the spices. Add the butter to the dry mixture, and blend until the mix looks like breadcrumbs. Stir in the sugar.

Lightly beat the egg and golden syrup together. Blend the two mixes together until they form a soft dough; you can use a food processor if you wish, to make it less hard on the arms. Tip the dough out and knead it until smooth. (This, *unfortunately*, cannot be achieved with a food processor.) Wrap it in clingfilm, and leave to chill in the fridge for 15 minutes.

Meanwhile, preheat the oven to 180°C / 350°F / Gas 4. Line two baking trays with greaseproof paper.

Roll the dough out to a 0.5cm/¼in thickness on a lightly floured surface. Cut out the gingerbread men shapes with the cutters you have to hand, and place on the baking tray. Be sure to leave a gap between each shape, as they'll expand during baking.

Bake for 12-15 minutes, or until lightly golden-brown.

Once the biscuits are cool, carefully take them to church, with a 1kg bag of icing sugar. Mix up 4 bowls of glacé icing (250g icing sugar, gradually, gradually add a trickle of water to make a thick paste). Provide many sugar based decorating things - we used silver balls, lots of different sprinkles, tubes of coloured piping icing, orange & lemon jelly slices and many more - paper plates to put finished saints on, and lots of baby wipes for cleaning sticky fingers.

St Mary At Stoke Gingerbread
- The Rev'd Simone Ramacci

I cannot claim this to be a family recipe, as it was kindly put through my letterbox by a lady from St Mary at Stoke, after I thoroughly enjoyed a slice or two following a Sunday service. I am yet to discover her name, but she has my thanks. I believe this recipe is from an old cookbook, with some changes.

Ingredients

4oz / 113g margarine
8oz / 226g golden syrup
¼ pint milk
2 eggs
1 tsp bicarbonate of soda
4oz / 113g plain flour
4oz / 113g wholewheat flour
2oz / 56g soft brown sugar
2 tsp mixed spice
3 tsp ground ginger
2oz / 56g crystallised ginger
2oz / 56g sultanas

Method

Brush a square tin with melted butter / margarine, cover with baking paper, and brush the paper too.

Heat the margarine together with the syrup in a saucepan, once melted take off the hob and add the milk, and beaten eggs. Combine the dry ingredients in a bowl, and mix in the liquid. Stir in the sultanas and crystallised ginger last.

Bake at 150°C (Gas mark 2) for 1h15m to 1h30m. You will know the bread is ready when the centre is springy and it begins to shrink away slightly from the side of the tin.

Economical Easter Biscuits
– Lyanne Brendt

My Mum got the Easter biscuits recipe when she was at school. She has one in her recipe for "Rich Easter Biscuits" which calls for lots of butter – and she's never made it as it's too expensive. But economical Easter biscuits mean "Easter" to me. The smell as they cook, and eating the little bits of raw dough that are trimmed off the edges... Yummy!

Ingredients

8oz / 226g flour
4oz / 113g sugar
4oz / 113g margarine
1½ tsp mixed spice
4-5oz / 113-141g currants
Little milk/egg yolk

Method

Cream margarine and sugar.

Sift flour and spice. Add currants. Mix.

Add milk or egg yolk as necessary to bind.

Roll out on a lightly floured surface. Cut and place on a buttered baking sheet.

Bake for 15-20 minutes at Gas 3 / 160°C.

Family Christmas Pudding
– Jean Brisland (courtesy of Chris Brisland)

<u>Ingredients</u>
½lb / 226g raisins
¾lb / 340g sultanas
¾lb / 340g currants
¼lb / 113g candied peel
2oz / 56g chopped blanched almonds
2oz / 56g glace cherries
½lb / 226g soft brown sugar
½lb / 226g soft white breadcrumbs
4oz / 113g plain flour
½lb / 226g chopped suet
Grated rind & juice of 1 lemon and 1 orange
1tsp mixed spice
½tsp salt
5 eggs
½ bottle of Guinness, barley wine, beer, ale, or milk
Optional: 1tbsp black treacle (if using, reduce sugar by 1oz)

For the brandy butter:
4oz / 113g unsalted butter
2oz / 56g caster sugar
6oz / 170g icing sugar
¾tbsp brandy

<u>Method</u>

Grease a 4pt pudding basin or equivalent. I use soft margarine and scatter sugar round.

Put a large pan/steamer to boil. Mix together all the clean, dried fruit. Chop or quarter cherries and mix with remaining dry ingredients. Make a well in the center of the ingredients and mix to a soft consistency with eggs, your chosen liquid, and lemon and orange juice.

Spoon into the prepared basin. Cover with foil and greaseproof paper or a pudding cloth, place in the pan/steamer, and put to cook for six hours. Make sure the water is always ¼ way up the basin, and refill with boiling water as necessary.

When cooked, remove the cover and allow to cool. Put a fresh cover on the top and keep pudding for several weeks until required. Reboil for at least 2hrs before serving. I tie round the foil with string to prevent water getting in; I also usually leave the foil etc on until they are cold and then replace them.

To make the brandy butter, soften the butter slightly and beat in the sugars. Beat in brandy according to taste.

Shortbread Biscuits
– Margaret Bloomfield

The reason why I like to make these biscuits is because they are very easy to make. They also hold together for my grandchildren to decorate. Also they are very short and crumbly to eat, so not too hard for your teeth!

Ingredients

325g / 11½oz plain flour
225g / 8oz lightly salted butter
110g / 4oz icing sugar

Method

Preheat the oven to fan 160° / electric 180° / Gas 4.

Either in a food processor or by hand, mix the ingredients together until you have a smooth dough.

Roll out the dough to about 5mm and cut into round shapes.

Bake on a lightly greased baking tray for about 10 minutes until lightly golden, allow to cool a little and transfer to a cooling rack.

Chocolate And Vanilla Cookies
– Lyanne Brendt

Chocolate and vanilla cookies mean Christmas and children, because this is a recipe I found when I needed to start making Christmas presents with little Rob and my little nephew. It's a lovely easy recipe to make with children, although they do get impatient about having to leave them in the fridge to firm up. I always plan to freeze at least one of the rolls of dough so we'll have some to eat another time... but it all gets eaten too soon!

Ingredients

Vanilla mix:
8oz / 226g butter (use a hard block, not softened spread)
12oz / 340g flour
6oz / 170g sugar
1 tsp baking powder
Few drops vanilla extract

Chocolate mix:
8oz / 226g butter (as above)
10oz / 283g flour
2oz / 56g cocoa
6oz / 170g sugar
1 tsp baking powder

Method

Soften butter and add other ingredients. Knead lightly.

Take quarter of each mix and squash together to form a roll. Repeat until you have 4 rolls. Chill for one hour.

Slice and bake in a pre-heated oven for 15 minutes at 180°C / Gas 4. Allow to cool for 5 minutes before removing to cooling racks.

Note: these spread whilst cooking.

Options – try chocolate and orange instead of vanilla.

Mincemeat Slice
– Carole Groom

Quick and easy tray bake.

Ingredients

2 large eggs
2 tsps vanilla essence
4oz / 110g soft margarine/spread
2oz / 55g sugar
4 dessert spoons mincemeat
6oz / 175g self raising flour
Traybake tin approx 11"x8" with baking parchment

Method

In a large bowl beat eggs and essence together.

Add all the other ingredients.

Beat well together for 2 minutes.

Line tray with baking parchment and spread the mixture evenly into tin.

Bake on bottom shelf at 150° fan / 325°F / Gas 3-4 for approx 25 minutes. Do not overbake. Cut into slices/square when cold.

Oat Fruit Slices
– Chris Fisher

Ingredients

6oz / 170g oats
6oz / 170g dried fruit eg dates, apricots, chopped raisins mixed together
¼ of 500g (125g / 4½oz) tub low fat buttery spread
2 tbs Demerara sugar (could replace one tbs with splenda granules)
3 tbs clear honey

Method

Melt in large saucepan over medium heat, stirring continually, until all the sugar is dissolved. Do not allow to boil.

Add dry ingredients to saucepan and mix thoroughly.

Put in shallow tin 17x22cm. Even out and press down firmly with back of spoon.

Bake in pre-heated oven 170°C / Gas 3 for approx 13mins (longer if not a fan oven). If your tin is slightly smaller, allow a little longer.

Allow to cool 10-15 minutes, then mark out in squares/oblongs. When completely cold, cut in shapes where marked.

Suggested variations:

Mixed dried fruit with cranberries and apricots – I found this in one of the supermarkets at Christmas time, also added ¼ tsp mixed spice.

6oz / 170g oats, 4oz / 113g grated mature cheddar, 2 oz / 57g apricots. Omit sugar and honey.

Cinnamon-Spiced Wedding Cookies
– Dale Cory

As typesetter and not church-goer, I'm hesistant to put my name to this recipe; but I do hope this is one the people of St Thomas's will appreciate regardless. I've always had something of a soft spot for these shortbread-esque cookies – moreish without lingering too long on the hips, and perfect for experimentation.

Ingredients

225g / 8oz butter, softened
50g / 2oz caster sugar
5ml / 1 teaspoon vanilla extract
225g / 8oz plain flour
115g / 4oz cornflour
50g / 2oz icing sugar
5ml / 1 teaspoon cinnamon (or whichever spice is preferred)

Method

Beat the butter with the caster sugar until light and fluffy. Add the vanilla extract.

Sift the flour and cornflour together over the mixture, then gradually work into the butter/sugar mixture until combined.

Roll heaped teaspoons of the mixture into balls and place on greased baking sheets.

Bake for 30 minutes at 160°C / Gas 3.

Sift the icing sugar and spice into a bowl. Toss the baked cookies in this mixture. Doing so when the cookies are completely cool ensures that they are more thoroughly covered, but you may prefer to do so when they are warm, if you want a different texture.

One can also stick squares of chocolate or pieces of fruit into the middle of each cookie before baking, if they so wish.

Go, eat your food with gladness, and drink your wine with a joyful heart, for God has already approved what you do.

ECCLESIASTES 9:7

Printed in Great Britain
by Amazon

13007367R00078